14-DAY FAITH MOVES DEVOTIONAL
FOR WOMEN EXPERIENCING INFERTILITY & LOSS

D. UPSHAW

Barren 2 Bearing: 14-Day Faith Moves Devotional For Women Experiencing Infertility & Loss

Copyright © 2019 DeVonna Upshaw

Books may be ordered by contacting:

Preemies & Bean Co. d/b/a Barren 2 Bearing
McDonough, GA 30253
www.barren2bearing.com

Cover art by EMBYRD DESIGNS™

Dedication

I dedicate this work to every BEARING woman who has stood in faith awaiting God's promise. "...Though it tarry, wait [earnestly] for it, because it will surely come; it will not be behindhand on its appointed day" (Hab 2:3, AMPC).

To the three men in my life that gave me the courage to pick up the pen and write, John Sr., John Jr. (Wes), & Rohen. You have given to me everything God promised, now I can give it to someone else.

To my Family & Friends, thank you for covering me and loving me enough to believe when I couldn't. It takes a village. We have two kings to raise!

To my spiritual parents Dr. Travis & Dr. Stephanie Jennings, thank you for speaking life to me, speaking life in me, and laying hands on me. Wednesday, November 1, 2017 will forever be etched in my heart.

Barren 2 Bearing:
14-Day Faith Moves Devotional
For Women Experiencing Infertility & Loss

A Glimpse Into Our Story

*"He gives the barren woman a home, making her the joyous mother of children. Praise the LORD!" -**Psalm 113:9 (ESV)***

My husband John and I were twenty years old the first time we were told by a doctor that having children biologically together would be difficult, if possible. As a woman, being told that my body may not be able to do what it had been created to do left me devastated, fearful, and full of uncertainty. How could THIS be the plan of God for my life? John and I were unmarried at the time of the news and I was unsure of what our next move would be, but luckily for me he was unmoved. Still, I'll never forgot the conversation John and I had after receiving this heart-breaking news. I had to tell a man who always joked about having five children because he came from a big family that if he chose to marry me still, his dreams of a family beyond the two of us may not be possible. Amazingly, this man with such a beautiful heart stood flat footed and told me with or without children he still chose me. We were married three years later.

Since then, the journey hasn't been easy. There were many private struggles that we didn't share with anyone. Several experimental procedures and a handful of diagnoses. The topic of children was "unofficially" banned In our house to protect my feelings in a season where my faith was fragile, and my belief was broken. For the first couple of years we never discussed it outside of doctor appointments. We had no idea what God had in store for us.

As we were leaving Bible Study on a Wednesday night in November 2017, our Pastor sensed the need to pray for women who wanted children. I honestly tried to get to the door and to our car as quickly as I could, but somehow, I ended up right in front of the altar where he was praying. I began to weep as my Pastor prayed. I had given up on the idea of children. I felt so defeated. This night was designed just for me, to restore my faith. The more he prayed, the more I felt strength to believe again.

That same night we conceived our son, John Westley Upshaw Jr. He was born premature but healthy on June 17, 2018, Father's Day. God made a believer out of me and I know He will do the same for you. Don't allow this present battle to place a period in your story where God has plans for a comma. We all have found ourselves in a faith fight with fertility, but even in our weakest moments, God's promises still stand!

3 | BARREN 2 BEARING

4|BARREN 2 BEARING

14-DAY FAITH MOVES DEVOTIONAL
FOR WOMEN EXPERIENCING INFERTILITY & LOSS

***Disclaimer**: In no way is this work intended to overlook the very serious struggles with infertility that many women face every day. I am also aware that not every woman experiencing infertility will mother a child biologically. Coupled with faith, please make sure you are taking the necessary dietary and medical steps instructed by medical professionals along this journey. Faith without works is dead, but God's promises aren't!*

No Room for DOUBT

*"Now Abraham and Sarah were old, well advanced in years; it had ceased to be with Sarah as with [young] women. [She was past the age of childbearing]. Therefore Sarah laughed to herself, saying, after I have become aged shall I have pleasure and delight, my lord (husband), being old also? And the Lord asked Abraham, Why did Sarah laugh, saying, Shall I really bear a child when I am so old? Is anything too hard or too wonderful for the Lord? At the appointed time, when the season [for her delivery] comes around, I will return to you and Sarah shall have borne a son." – **Genesis 18:11-14 Amplified Bible, Classic Edition (AMPC)**

Sarah laughed at the thought of conceiving a child in her old age. In her own eyes, she was past her childbearing years and too worn out from life to even consider such a notion. Imagine being told by God that the very thing you've prayed for the most is getting ready to show up in your life and instead of being consumed by joy, you're burdened and weighed down with doubt. That's exactly what happened to Sarah. She was in her nineties when God told Abraham that within a year, she would bear him a son. The very prayer she had been praying all these years had finally been answered, yet no celebration ensued. She found herself laughing at the promise instead of praising God for His faithfulness. What do you do when knowing just isn't enough? Now you are forced to believe!

We all can relate to Sarah's plight. Many of us have prayed, received prayer, and have even heard the voice of God reassuring us that He would do just what He said, however believing to the point of manifestation can be much easier said than done. God himself appeared before Abraham and told him what would take place, Sarah even heard it as she eavesdropped on their conversation, yet she still struggled with doubt and unbelief to the point of laughter. If you're anything like me, laughter wasn't the reaction given the first time someone told me God would honor our prayers and give my husband and I a child. First, there was joy. Almost immediately following that came brokenness, anger, weariness, grief, and yes doubt. Doubt would often consume me. If I can be completely honest, it becomes very cumbersome to continuously hear about what God is "going" to do when you've been waiting a while for Him to do it. If you're not careful, you will even begin to despise the very words of encouragement you've received.

What I've learned in this process is that there is a big difference between *knowing* and *believing*. Sarah knew God said that she would bear a child in her old age, but she struggled believing that it could happen. Doubt is a subtle enemy. It creeps in unknowingly and can often distract you from what God has promised you. Amongst many things, God has promised me that my entire family will know Him and be saved, however believing based on what I currently see can be difficult. I *know* He can do it yet believing Him for the manifestation hasn't always been easy. With that I am reminded of something my Pastor often says, **"We are not moved by what we see, ONLY by what we believe"** (2 Corin 5:7). Doubt has no room for what you are believing God for. To deal with our doubts, we must submit our hearts to God's word and hold on to it despite our difficult circumstances. You must completely evict doubt from your mind, heart, and spirit and fully receive God's love for you. The Bible says we are transformed and effectively changed when we renew and rejuvenate our minds (Rom 12:2). We are no longer broken barren women with an issue; we are **BEARING BELIEVING** women with a promise and a purpose!

A Prayer of Faith

Lord, I thank you for helping me cancel doubt and fear in my life despite what I've endured. According to Mark 11:24, you said if I confidently believe and not doubt in the things I have prayed for, it will be given to me. I believe that just as you did it for Sarah, so will you do it for me. Today, I make a conscious decision to stand in faith and not fear. I am no longer barren, I am bearing. Amen!

Notes

_____

_____

_____

_____

_____

_____

_____

DAY **2**

FAITH MOVES

We have all been guilty of doubt at one point in our life. Take some time to rejuvenate your mind and be intentional about what you are believing God for. Where God is getting ready to take you and your family, doubt can't come. Make an honest and detailed list of some of the doubts that have been holding you back. Once the list is complete, take a few every day and commit them to prayer. Be sure to keep track of your progress in your *Faith Moves Journal*.

DAY 3

They Just Don't Get It

"[This embarrassed and grieved Hannah] and her rival provoked her greatly to vex her, because the Lord had left her childless. So it was year after year; whenever Hannah went up to the Lord's house, Peninnah provoked her, so she wept and did not eat. Then Elkanah her husband said to her, Hannah, why do you cry? And why do you not eat? And why are you grieving? Am I not more to you than ten sons? So Hannah rose after they had eaten and drunk in Shiloh. Now Eli the priest was sitting on his seat beside a post of the temple (tent) of the Lord. And [Hannah] was in distress of soul, praying to the Lord and weeping bitterly." – **1 Sam 1:6-10 Amplified Bible, Classic Edition (AMPC)**

The emotional distress that I felt month after month of learning that we had not conceived is one I can barely place into words. It was undeniably one of the hardest things I've gone through in life. 1 Samuel says that Hannah was "in distress of soul", meaning her mind, her will, her emotions, and her conscious understanding were all effected by the pain and anguish she felt. Unlike Sarah, Hannah was still well within her childbearing years and all she desired was a son of her own. Unfortunately, not only had she not yet conceived, she also had to endure being taunted and bullied by Peninnah for being barren. Peninnah's taunts even followed her as she went to the Lord's house to worship. Her husband Elkanah passionately and unconditionally loved his wife Hannah for who she was and who she currently wasn't. He could not understand why she would allow her *temporary* inability to bare him a child cause her such grief and inner turmoil.

My husband was just like Elkanah. Many women can relate to this; whether it be your spouse, a family member, or a friend. It's something about the personal experience and struggle of trying to conceive that can only be explained and felt by the person facing the problem. My husband wasn't the issue, I was, but he loved me for all of me with or without a child. I believe it was my warped view of that love that often made him come across as insensitive to what I was dealing with. In no way was he harsh or rude, he was extremely supportive, but he just didn't get it. He didn't understand why I would cry and fall into a semi-depression every time I started my menstrual cycle. He couldn't comprehend the fear and anxiety I felt every time I would take a pregnancy test. He didn't get why I would torture myself by purchasing baby clothes and other items week after week only to give them away in my distress. In his mind he loved me, and he knew and believed without a doubt what God said He would do. That's what he allowed to comfort and keep him when we received bad news. He knew that no matter what we were presently experiencing, all things were STILL working together for our good (Rom 8:28). In hindsight, I'm thankful that he remained steadfast at times when I couldn't. It was his faith that I leaned on for strength to pull me out month after month.

I learned that some people won't get it—and that's perfectly fine. They are not supposed to. This faith walk is something between you and God and He's teaching you to trust Him even when you cannot trace Him. Your spouse, your family, and even your friends love you and want to see the promises of God take place in your life. Don't take any of their misinformed emotions personally because they are simply that, misinformed. You will surely testify of God's goodness in the end and they will all be there to celebrate with you. Spiritually, you are bearing more than you know and that is the breeding grounds for a miracle designed just for **YOU**.

A Prayer of Faith

Lord, thank you for understanding my grief and hearing my prayers. I know in my heart that my family and friends want to see God's promises revealed in my life. Help me not to take this faith fight personal, but instead teach me to lean on you for my strength (2 Corin. 12:9). They may not get it, but you see me, and you do. Amen!

Notes

_____

_____

_____

_____

_____

_____

_____

FAITH MOVES

Naturally as humans we look for comfort from the ones closest to us in times of grief and despair. No need to beat yourself up there, it's normal. Some things *can* be worked out that way, however there are other times when *only* God can heal you where you are hurting. All you have to do is invite Him in.

As you journey through this devotional schedule a specific time every day where you can be intimate and vulnerable with God. Tell Him all about the hopelessness you are feeling. He completely gets it and wants you to come to Him so that He can comfort you (Matt 11:28). Be sure to write down any instructions He gives you in your ***Faith Moves Journal***.

I ~~Don't~~ DO Mind Waiting

*"The Lord does not delay and is not tardy or slow about what He promises, according to some people's conception of slowness, but He is long-suffering (extraordinarily patient) toward you..." – **2 Peter 3:9 Amplified Bible, Classic Edition (AMPC)***

Often it is not that we haven't placed our faith and trust in God, it is that we have not done so long or openly enough. Long-suffering is a word no one likes to hear in times of distress and brokenness; however, its attributes are fruitful and life giving, both spiritually and naturally. "The wait" is undeniably one of the hardest parts of the process. This part has nothing to do with doubt. Instead, it has everything to do with building patience and endurance. I've learned that God is a perfect gentleman in every way. He never forces Himself into any situation. He only shows up by open invitation. Sometimes during our grief we forget to invite Him into what's ailing us, and in our frustration, we revert to doubt and even complaining. 2 Peter 3:9 says that He is "extraordinarily patient" towards us, meaning He doesn't mind waiting on us to get it right. Ask yourself this, "If He doesn't mind, why should I?"

When you lack patience, complaining may seem like a great let out to your frustration, but it does much more damage than good. It is pleasing to God when we fully trust in Him without complaining (Phil. 2:13-14). Complaining not only releases negativity into the atmosphere, it also causes you to have to redo milestones God has already carried you through. This can further your frustration. Remember, God can only participate when He is invited to do so. There is so much power in the things we say; make sure your words are life giving and not destructive (Prov. 18:21). Easier said than done I know, but worth the effort. There were days when I allowed complaining to overtake me. I was full of self-pity and completely hopeless. It wasn't until I came across the promise in Psalm 113:9 that I completely changed my outlook on the difficulties to conceive. I found myself asking for forgiveness for not being patient as God had been patient with me. I found God's plan for me written in that Psalm and realized that He already had a fully planned out ending to my suffering and it was one of joy, happiness, and family (Jer. 29:11).

In learning and accepting patience throughout this process, I also learned that a part of patience is letting go. No, not letting go of your desire to have a child and a family. You have to let go of the control you think you have over the situation. Notice I said **think**. God is and has always been in complete control from the beginning. I had to stop obsessing over the idea of getting pregnant. I had to stop allowing the anxieties of bad news to consume me month after month. At one point, I completely stopped mentioning having a baby all together. Letting go almost felt like losing in the beginning, but I learned that in leaning on God and truly waiting on Him there's renewed strength and fortitude (Isa. 40:31). Don't be afraid to give your baby to God, even before he/she are even conceived. He is a good good Father. He will not forsake nor disappoint you.

A Prayer of Faith

Lord, thank you for giving me the grace to be patient. I fully understand that I am not in control here, you are! Even though it is difficult for me to envision the outcome, I know the ending will be GOOD (Jer. 29:11)! Teach me to wait on you just like you've waited on me. I will no longer handle patience as an option, but instead I'll treat it as a virtue. Amen!

Notes

_____

_____

_____

_____

FAITH MOVES

Waiting can seem unbearable at times but know that being patient produces character and with character, HOPE (Rom 5:3-4). Take the worry out of your wait and give it all to God. I encourage you to go back and reflect on the story of Hannah in 1 Samuel 1. She too wasn't thrilled with the idea of waiting, but she invited God into her situation and in her wait, she found victory and breakthrough. Be sure to jot down any notes and reflections in your *Faith Moves Journal*.

Think On These Things

*"Summing it all up, friends, I'd say you'll do best by filling your minds and meditating on things true, noble, reputable, authentic, compelling, gracious—the best, not the worst; the beautiful, not the ugly; things to praise, not things to curse." – **Philippians 4:8 The Message (MSG)***

We addressed renewing the mind on Day 1 when we waived doubt and unbelief goodbye (so long bye, bye). The word "renewing" is a verb, an action word. To RE-new means to continuously make fresh again and that's what you have to do with your mind. You must consistently infuse your mind with the word of God which breeds new and refreshing thought patterns. Meditating or focusing one's thoughts on a specific idea or goal can be beneficial to your mental health. Let's face it, we've all had those days where this journey of faith and obedience has caused us to want to give up. Finding scriptures or an encouraging message to meditate on during those rough times can bring great comfort.

I was watching *"The Heather Lindsey Show"* on The Word Network the first time I heard Psalm 113:9.

I had never tuned in to the show before and somehow stumbled across it that day. There were two women on her show sharing their testimonies of victory over infertility. As soon as I heard the topic being discussed I was instantly annoyed. I wasn't at all interested in hearing anything they had to say. I was currently in a slump having one of "those days" and didn't care to be entertained by someone else's fairytale. For some odd reason though, I didn't turn it off. Unbeknownst to me, there was a divine reason why I had tuned in. As one of the ladies began to speak, she spoke on how she would read Psalm 113:9 and the encouragement and comfort it provided. I had never heard of it before, so I pulled out my phone and looked it up while still tuning in. As I read it in multiple versions, I could literally feel the love of God wrapping itself around me. Ha! I didn't even want to watch the show, but God snuck something in there just for ME! Immediately, I wrote the scripture down and placed it on my vanity so that I could see it and meditate on it daily. On the days where I couldn't seem to shake the heaviness, this scripture would literally lighten the load. It was like I could hear God saying, "think on this, let this remind you of my promise." I am amazed by His grace and love for me, even when I closed myself up to receiving it.

Meditating can keep you from self-medicating. Meditation is used and viewed differently amongst various religious groups and worldviews. Meditating on the word of God is vital for a prosperous life and it fuels effective prayer (Jos 1:8). It is very important to find yourself in the scripture and let that fuel you. When you have become so full of His word, there is no room for stinking thinking and pity parties. You find strength in knowing what He said. I know this because I've lived it. On the days where my "reality" was too much I thought about His promise in the word and held on to that truth! He wants to make me a happy mother of children. He wants to restore joy to my house. He finds good pleasure in doing what He said (Luke 12:32). Think on those things that match what God has said about you and before you know it, you'll be living it!

A Prayer of Faith

Lord, rid me of my stinking thinking concerning your promises for my life. Teach me not to shut out your word but to embrace it and the life it gives. Instead of complaining, I will meditate on your word and allow it to be my fuel. I am who you said I am. Amen!

Notes

_____

_____

FAITH MOVES

Meditating can keep you from self-medicating. I've read many stories of women who turned to alternative methods to numb the pains of infertility. Luckily, that doesn't have to be your story. I know many of you may already have scriptures of choice that you meditate on, but I want to encourage you to add Psalm 113:9 to your list. For the next 21 days (it has been proven that a new habit can become a lifestyle in a consistent 21-day period), read Psalm 113:9 every morning out loud before you start your day and then just be silent for a moment. Allow the word to embed itself in your spirit and watch God's love overtake you. Use your **Faith Moves Journal** to write down your reflections from this time of meditation.

*"He gives the barren woman a home, making her the joyous mother of children. Praise the LORD!" -**Psalm 113:9 (ESV)***

Practice the Practical

*"So do not worry or be anxious about tomorrow, for tomorrow will have worries and anxieties of its own. Sufficient for each day is its own trouble." – **Matthew 6:34 Amplified Bible, Classic Edition (AMPC)***
****
*"When you embrace the uncertain, life opens up unusual new paths. Seeds sown way back bloom as flowers, in ways one can never fathom." -**Subroto Bagchi***

Live in the moment, brave the day, make the most of the present time and give little thought to the future. Carpe diem, Seize the day! It sounds a bit insensitive from the place of hopelessness; however, there's so much freedom and empowerment in the practical steps of the process. Although many things are connected spiritually, some things are very practical. Practicality is the intentional forward movement of experienced living without deeply analyzing every move. Find things, people, and places that make you happy and cultivates your vibe daily. It is so easy for our focus to be consumed by what we don't have but try living and enjoying what you do. Before you know it those seeds of happiness will bloom into flowers of joy.

God promises us daily bread, meaning He will give us exactly what we need to make it through the current because it is He who holds the future and has it already planned out (Jer. 29:11). All God is asking us to do is, LIVE! I remember days when I literally had to force myself out of the bed and out of the house. Depression was on me like a shadow and I felt like I couldn't shake it. I prayed and even fasted for God to heal my broken heart and the bitterness I felt from not yet being pregnant, but still on many days I couldn't shake those feelings. I wasn't braving the day at all. I was allowing my day to have its way with me instead of me commanding my day. It wasn't until I read a scripture that I always hear my Pastor say with a new mindset that I was able to really break free from a cycle of self-bullying. Job 38:12-13(NIV) says, ***"Have you ever given orders to the morning, or shown the dawn its place, that it might take the earth by the edges and shake the wicked out of it?"*** Am I saying that you can choose what kind of day you have just by being intentional? YES! Get up, put some uplifting music on, get dressed, do your hair, wear that favorite lip color of yours, stop by the mall for some light shopping, go see that movie you've been wanting to see, or call your friends for a girl's day. Whatever it takes, just make sure you're the one taking it and making it yours!

Embracing the uncertain is much easier said than done. It is foreign and scary territory to tread. It takes much strength to live in the moment when the current feels unpleasant. The great news is we don't have to rely on our own strength (2 Corin. 12:9). Pull on the strength of the Lord to brave your day and don't forget to reward yourself when you do. Take the anxieties and pressures of tomorrow and shake them out of your today. Seize every opportunity to live and live WELL! As Dr. Travis Jennings would say, *"Your current condition is not your concrete conclusion."* Live for today, because tomorrow is already planned out.

A Prayer of Faith

Lord, teach me to be balanced in both the spiritual and the practical. Help me to be intentional about my joy and seek after happiness daily. Every day is a day that you have made. Not only should I rejoice and be glad in it, but I should also seize it. Today, I shake everything contrary to your promises out of my life and make a conscious decision to LIVE and live well. Amen!

Notes

_____

_____

_____

FAITH MOVES

We are taking back our joy, our peace, and our sanity. It is not God's will for you to suffer while waiting on the promise. Plan a day of fun for the upcoming weekend. You may not feel up to it, but a day with your spouse, your family, or your friends is just what you need. Every time something negative tries to distract you, shut it down. Be sure you reflect on your day in your **Faith Moves Journal**. Make it a habit to plan more days like this soon.

DAY 11

It's BIGGER Than You Think

*"[Not in your own strength] for it is God Who is all the while effectually at work in you [energizing and creating in you the power and desire], both to will and to work for His good pleasure and satisfaction and delight." – **Philippians 2:13 Amplified Bible, Classic Edition (AMPC)***

Even though it doesn't feel like it, God is working overtime on your behalf. Believe it or not, He desires this child just as much as you do. Why? Because your child already has a purpose and destiny and it is for God's good pleasure, satisfaction, and delight. When you think of it that way, it becomes much easier to believe that God will open your womb and give you a child. He is effectively at work behind every tear, every negative pregnancy test, and every discouraging thought. That's extremely encouraging to the discouraged! Don't compare your process to others or give up because someone seems to be further along in the process. Everyone's process is different. Trust God in yours; not in your own strength, but in the strength of the Lord.

Before I renewed my faith in becoming pregnant, because I also went through a phase of giving up, I had to go through an entire mental and spiritual shift. The way I was viewing my current predicament wasn't healthy or helping. I changed the way I perceived God in my mind and in my heart. I was begging Him for a child because "I" wanted one, but never once did I consider why He wanted to give me one. This desire that I had was much bigger than me, because it was God himself giving and working it in me. That was my "ah ha" moment. The desire to have this child was for God's glory. I was going to be a mother, but God was going to be the Father. Your child coming into the earth will serve a far greater purpose than you know. Their entrance will bring about another level of faith, healing, and restoration to your family. It's okay to *feel* lost and alone in this, as long as you know that you're *never* alone.

Consider the story of Abraham. Abraham married Sarah. Sarah was barren. They eventually had a son named Isaac. Isaac married Rebekah. Rebekah was barren. They eventually had a son named Jacob. Jacob married Rachel. Rachel was barren. They eventually had a son named Joseph. God's promise to Abraham was to make him the "father of many nations" with countless descendants, yet all these men from his lineage dealt with infertility through their wives. Do you see a pattern here? The IMPOSSIBILITY factor was a part of God's fulfillment and it brought Him so much glory.

Wherever you may be in this journey, whether you've been trying for one year or several years to conceive, God heard your petition the first time. Not only did He hear it, but it is HE who imparted those desires in you. He's going to honor your request. I've learned that God's timing is perfect and not a second before His "set time" will do. I'm again reminded of Hannah. She wanted to give her husband a child, not knowing who this child would end up being. It was the Lord who had closed Hannah's womb (1 Sam. 1:5). He knew this child had a purpose and needed to come at the perfect time. Your child has a perfect arrival time as well. No one having fertility issues wants to hear that, myself included, but it doesn't stop it from being the truth. Creation is awaiting your child's arrival. Embrace the promises AND the timing of God. Remember it is God who is creating the power and desire in you. He has His hands on your promise and won't let it go until He can hand deliver it to you. Trust that He's a big God, who can do big things, much BIGGER than we can imagine ask for or think (Eph. 3:20).

A Prayer of Faith

Lord, forgive me for being selfish in my desires. I know that my child will serve a greater purpose just like Samuel. Help me to see the bigger picture. This child has been chosen by you before I've even conceived it (Jer. 1:5). You hold the future because you created it. I trust that your plan is perfect and designed just for me. Amen!

Notes

_____

_____

_____

_____

_____

_____

_____

DAY 12

FAITH MOVES

It's much BIGGER than you can imagine. God's plan for the expansion of your family is fully in the works. Say this prayer, *"Lord, I release my control and give you complete control. I know you've heard my petition the first time and it is your desire to answer it in your perfect timing. I now know that conceiving is much bigger than me, it is for your glory. I know you will never forsake me. God, I trust your process, Amen!"*. Just like that you've shifted. Now be silent in His presence and allow God to wrap His reassuring arms around you. Jot down anything you hear God saying during your time with him in your *Faith Moves Journal*.

Faith Moves

"Sing, barren woman, who has never had a baby. Fill the air with song, you who've never experienced childbirth! You're ending up with far more children than all those childbearing women. God says so!" – Isaiah 54:1 The Message (MSG)

Sing! Sing! Sing because you've gone from barren to BEARING! You may not yet be pregnant, but your spirit is. It's bearing your promise. You've allowed God to shift your mind and heart concerning what He promised you. Prepare for your womb to be opened in God's perfect timing. You're going to end up far happier than you could have ever imagined. Your faith has stood the test of time and disappointment. This is something to celebrate. You may still be in the process, yet now you are confident in the outcome. God was speaking to Israel in Isaiah 54:1. Although they were not yet out of captivity, God was telling them to celebrate and rejoice NOW because He was getting ready to set them free. You may not have the physical manifestation yet, but your faith in what God promised has leveled up. Now it's time to take it a step further. Faith moves is faith in action.

When my husband and I were believing God for our first home, we encountered major setbacks and disappointments along the way. As a matter of fact, we were told no by several lenders for the house that we live in now. We found the house and fell in love with it. On our way out of town to a family reunion we stopped, signed the paperwork, and placed the earnest money down. By the time we made it to our destination, the lender called back and told us to go get our money back because we would not be able to purchase this house. Heartbroken and devastated, I cried in the car while my husband checked us into our hotel. We ended up at a local shopping center the next day and as we were walking around, I heard the Lord say, "purchase something for your new home". It literally stopped me in my tracks. Why would God tell me to purchase something for a house we were just told it was impossible for us to get? I immediately shared it with my husband who through disappointment was a bit skeptical himself. We ultimately decided to trust God at His word anyway and purchased something for our new home. That was in May. We closed on the house we were told was impossible for us to purchase in October of that same year. God was faithful to His word.

Though the process of believing God for our house wasn't easy, we kept exercising our faith. Every time we received discouraging news we would go and purchase something for the house. Everything from curtains to flatware were purchased before we ever got a yes. So, with that same concept of faith, I challenge you to make a FAITH MOVE. If you're anything like me, you've already picked out the room in your home that will ultimately become your baby's nursery. If you haven't, choose one. I challenge you, you and your husband together, to go purchase something for your baby and place it in the room. It can be something as simple as our "Psalm 113:9" onesie available for purchase on our website. Whatever you choose, take it and place it where it would go when baby arrives. Spend time in the room frequently together. Every time you feel discouraged or receive not so good news, add another item to your nursery because a *Faith Move* will move your faith from stuck to standing on His word. Sing you BEARING woman, your promise is on the way, you've got this!

A Prayer of Faith

Lord, I BELIEVE! I stand on Amos 9:13 knowing it won't be long now. I choose to step out in faith and make a Faith Move towards my family's future. I trust your word. Thank you for hearing my prayers. Amen!

Notes

_____

_____

_____

_____

_____

_____

_____

DAY 14

FAITH MOVES

This has been an amazing and life changing journey together. You are now ready to finish walking out what God said. In your *Faith Moves Journal*, both you and your spouse together prepare daily declarations for your child that are affirming, full of purpose, spirit-filled, and life giving. Be sure to make reading them out loud a part of your daily routine.

Infertility In The Bible

Infertility and the faith to believe is so near to God's heart that it is presented within the first few chapters of the Bible. Below are a few of those stories.

Abraham + Sarah

Abraham and Sarah's story of infertility is probably the most well known in scripture. In Genesis 17:15, God spoke to Abraham and told him that Sarah would bear him a son. Sarah was well beyond child-bearing years when she conceived and gave birth to their son Isaac. Their entire story can be found in **Genesis 15-21**.

Isaac + Rebekah

When Isaac was forty years old he married Rebekah. Isaac prayed to the Lord on behalf of his wife Rebekah because she was barren. God answered his prayers. Not only did He heal her barrenness, God blessed them with twin boys, Esau and Jacob. **Genesis 25:20-24**.

Jacob + Rachel

Jacob married both Rachel and her sister Leah. While Leah was able to conceive six sons, Rachel remained childless. After much bitterness, brokenness, and feeling like she was in competition with Leah, God remembered Rachel and opened her womb. She gave birth to Joseph and later Benjamin. **Genesis 29-30**.

Hannah + Elkanah

Hannah wanted nothing more than to give her husband Elkanah a son. Her barrenness completely wore her down. Hannah wept for a son and after several years, God honored her request. She gave birth to the Prophet Samuel (and later five more children). **1 Samuel 1**.

Manoah + His Wife

Manoah's wife was barren. An angel of the Lord appeared to her and told her she would conceive and give birth to a son. She was also given specific dietary instructions to follow. Manoah's wife conceived and gave birth to Samson later known for his supernatural strength. **Judges 13**.

The Shunammite Woman + Her Husband

The Shunammite woman and her husband opened their home for lodging to the Prophet Elisha whenever he would pass through. Because of their hospitality, Elisha asked what could he do for them. The woman was barren. She expressed her desire to conceive a son even though her husband was old. Elisha prophesied to her that within a year she would hold a child in her arms. Within a year she gave birth to a son. **2 Kings 4:8-17**.

Elisabeth + Zacharias

Just like Sarah, Elisabeth was barren and beyond her child-bearing years. Zacharias, her husband, prayed in the temple of the Lord. Suddenly, an angel of the Lord appeared before him and told him that his wife would bear him a son. Elisabeth later gave birth to John the Baptist. **Luke 1:5-25**.

I have been created to be fruitful and multiply. (Gen. 1:28, Ps 113:9)

Lord, I thank you for giving me a family making me to be a joyful mother of children.

My prayers have been heard by God, He honors my sacrifice, and I WILL conceive. (1 Sam 1:10-20)

Lord, thank you that in my grief and despair, you heard my cry.

My womb has been abundantly blessed to prosper and bare children. (Gen 49:25)

Lord, I thank you for giving me life in my womb and causing me to prosper.

I will carry my child full-term without any complications. (Phil 1:6)

Lord, I thank you that what you've begun in my womb, you'll complete and make perfect.

My baby will be healthy blessed and a reward from the Lord. (Psalm 127:3)

Lord, I thank you for building legacy in my womb.

I will not be governed or emotionally swayed by the opinions of doctors when I know who holds the future of my seed. (Jer. 29:11, 32:27)

Lord, I thank you for having an expected end for my family and I which includes children.

Not only will you answer my prayers to conceive, you will continue to honor them and bless the generations to come after me. (Deut. 7:14)

Lord, I thank you for making my lineage fruitful and canceling barrenness for generations to come.

AMEN, and it is so!

Genesis 1:28: "Then God blessed them and said, 'Be fruitful and multiply. Fill the earth and govern it. Reign over the fish in the sea, the birds in the sky, and all the animals that scurry along the ground." (NLT)

Genesis 49:25: "By the God of your father, Who will help you, and by the Almighty, Who will bless you with blessings of the heavens above, blessings lying in the deep that couches beneath, blessings of the breasts and of the womb." (AMPC)

Deuteronomy 7:14: "You shall be blessed above all peoples; there shall not be male or female barren among you, or among your cattle." (AMPC)

Deuteronomy 28:2-6: "You will experience all these blessings if you obey the Lord your God: Your towns and your fields will be blessed. Your children and your crops will be blessed. The offspring of your herds and flocks will be blessed. Your fruit baskets and breadboards will be blessed. Wherever you go and whatever you do, you will be blessed." (NLT)

Psalm 84:11: "For the Lord God is our sun and our shield. He gives us grace and glory. The Lord will withhold no good thing from those who do what is right." (NLT)

Psalm 113:9: "He gives the barren woman a home, making her the joyous mother of children. Praise the LORD!" (ESV)

Psalm 127:3: "Behold, children are a heritage from the Lord, the fruit of the womb a reward." (AMPC)

Psalm 128:1-4: "How joyful are those who fear the Lord—all who follow his ways! You will enjoy the fruit of your labor. How joyful and prosperous you will be! Your wife will be like a fruitful grapevine, flourishing within your home. Your children will be like vigorous young olive trees as they sit around your table. That is the Lord's blessing for those who fear him." (NLT)

Jeremiah 32:27: "Behold, I am the Lord, the God of all flesh; is there anything too hard for Me?" (AMPC)

John 16:24: "Up to this time you have not asked a [single] thing in My Name [as presenting all that I Am]; but now ask and keep on asking and you will receive, so that your joy (gladness, delight) may be full and complete." (AMPC)

Romans 2:11: "For God shows no partiality [undue favor or unfairness; with Him one man is not different from another]." (AMPC)

Hebrews 11:1: "Now faith is the assurance (the confirmation, the title deed) of the things [we] hope for, being the proof of things [we] do not see and the conviction of their reality [faith perceiving as real fact what is not revealed to the senses]." (AMPC)

Hebrews 11:11: "Because of faith also Sarah herself received physical power to conceive a child, even when she was long past the age for it, because she considered [God] Who had given her the promise to be reliable and trustworthy and true to His word." (AMPC)

Mark 11:24: "For this reason I am telling you, whatever you ask for in prayer, believe (trust and be confident) that it is granted to you, and you will [get it]." (AMPC)

Genesis 25:21: "Isaac prayed to the LORD on behalf of his wife, because she was childless. The LORD answered his prayer, and his wife Rebekah became pregnant." (NIV)

Jeremiah 1:5: "Before I formed you in the womb I knew you, before you were born I set you apart; I appointed you as a prophet to the nations." (NIV)

About The Author

D. Upshaw is a Momprenuer and the founder of Preemies & Bean Co., a company built on bringing awareness to premature birth and infertility amongst women. Born and raised in Rochester, N.Y., D. has always aspired to influence, impact, and encourage her generation as well as the next. She is charismatic, compassionate, creative, and capable of doing everything she sets her mind and heart to do. She serves faithfully in her local church and lends her gifts, talents, and skills when needed to serve others.

D. currently resides in Atlanta, GA with her devoted and equally creative husband, John Sr., and their two amazing little boys John Jr. (Wes) & Rohen.

For more information about our story, stop by www.barren2bearing.com.

Made in the
USA
Lexington, KY